Life Insurance...
Who Needs It?

What Life Insurance Agents May Not Tell You...
But You Need To Know... Before You Buy

By
Keith Maderer

Part of the:

Life Insurance...
Who Needs It?

What Life Insurance Agents May Not Tell You...
But You Need To Know... Before You Buy

By
Keith Maderer

Part of the:
K.I.S.S.S.
Keeping It Simple - Single Solutions
S E R I E S

All Rights Reserved - Worldwide
Copyright © 2017 by Keith Maderer

Website:
KeithMaderer.com
Amazon Author Page

ISBN-13: 978-1537470788
ISBN-10: 1537470787

ALL RIGHTS RESERVED. This book contains material protected under International and Federal Copyright Laws and Treaties. Any unauthorized reprint or use of this material is prohibited. No part of this publication may be reproduced or transmitted in any manner whatsoever without express written permission of the author/publisher, except for brief quotations embodied in critical articles or reviews.

Special Bonus Offer

Get your

Free Chapter and Author Video:
WARNING: Stuff That Pisses Me Off About Life Insurance

Get yours by clicking here:

http://kdmaderer.evsuite.com/life-insurance/

Introduction:

The Problem...

That life insurance sales person is calling me... again.

He was referred by my friend Jim (or cousin, or parents or whoever else).

He wants to come over to the house and... "share some great ideas to help me".

I need some additional protection, but I have no idea how much. What company or what type insurance I should buy remain a mystery.

I am married and we recently had our first child... a beautiful baby girl named Stephanie.

We bought our first house and the mortgage payments are manageable. I don't have... or want to spend a lot of money on something like life insurance.

Every year, millions of young couples experience these exact same thoughts.

Every year, millions of high-cost life insurance policies are **sold** to those same unsuspecting young families by highly-trained sales people.

Some go door to door. Others try using guilt and high-pressure tactics while sitting across from you at your own kitchen table. They even double-team you, by bringing another sales person with them.

If any of these situations sound familiar... you need to read on.

The Solution...

Great news... today you will find out how to avoid these

uncomfortable situations. This book will give you all the information you need. Find out what kind of insurance is best for you and your family... how much you need and should purchase... the best companies to get it from... where to get it, and how to get the lowest possible cost to fit within your budget.

Sure Keith... that sounds great. How do I know you aren't trying to sell me a bunch of bull??

Why Believe Me??

Let me give you a little bit of my background. I have been a "Fee-Only" financial adviser for over 25 years. Fee-only means that my clients pay me directly for the advice I give them. I do not receive any compensation or commissions from other sources. I do receive a small royalty from the books I have written. Check out my **Amazon Author Page** to see other titles - http://amazon.com/author/keithmaderer)

I have been in the financial advisory business for over 35 years.

Yes... I started at IDS/American Express, which is now Ameriprise Financial.

Yes... I was trained to sell life insurance, annuities, mutual funds, limited partnerships, and other financial investments.

Yes... I was taught the guilt and pressure sales techniques.

Yes... I was paid commissions for selling the products of the companies we used.

Yes... I left and started my own company and it has grown and prospered over the past 25 years because I took a different approach. Instead of being paid commissions by companies to push their products. I chose to sell my advice to clients. I work for you... not the insurance, annuity or investment companies.

You hire me... I work for you. I help you find the best insurance, investments, and financial advice at the lowest possible costs... without conflicts of interest. I am not beholden to any company because they pay my income. You do... my client.

By purchasing this book, you and I make an investment in each other. You pay a small price for this book... I offer my years of experience and best advice so you can find the best deal for yourself.

My clients pay hundreds, thousands and even tens of thousands of dollars each year for my comprehensive advice and guidance with their overall financial, retirement, tax and estate concerns. You get one specific area of this knowledge... for less than the cost of a dinner.

You will save thousands of dollars over the years and help your family achieve better financial results. You will avoid uncomfortable, stressful situations, and enjoy peace of mind. This book is a short read, without the usual fluff.

I have helped hundreds of young couples, including my own children, family, friends, and clients find the best insurance at the lowest possible cost.

I previously taught the licensing course for Life, Health and Accident insurance at a local college, until I realized how boring that was.

My Promise to You...

I promise... you can... and will be able to find the right type of life insurance. You will find the best companies and the lowest cost policy for you and your family.

If, after reading this book, you disagree, I will refund your entire cost.

Just send me an email at keith@keithmaderer.com . Send a copy of your paid receipt for the book along with your name, address and phone number. I will send you a full refund.

Yes... I am that confident that you **can** do it.

Take Action Now...

Don't wait until that salesperson knocks on your door... or worse yet, they are sitting at your kitchen table. Arm yourself with the knowledge and resources to find the right company, the right amount, and the best price.

The process is not rocket science, but you do need to know what to look for before you are taken advantage of. Each chapter gives you insight into making the best decisions for you and your family.

Spend a few dollars now to save thousands over the coming years. The money you save will help you with your child's education, your retirement or just buying a new car or dining room table. You decide... don't allow yourself to be taken advantage of. Take control of your life... and enjoy the peace of mind knowing you made a great decision.

Your Challenge...

This book will challenge you to take a series of small steps that will educate and entertain you each step of the way. Your challenge is to complete each chapter and finish this short book. Then acquire the right type, correct amount, best riders and lowest cost life insurance policy to meet you and your growing family's needs.

Don't let anyone tell you... you cannot do it. Each chapter will guide you through another step of the process. There are 7 chapters, 7 attainable mini-goals, 7 items on your checklist to accomplish.

I believe in you and your ability to change. Don't let me, or more importantly... your loved ones... down.

Table of Contents

Special Bonus Offer..3

Introduction:..5

Why I Wrote This Book..10

Who Should Read This Book...11

Chapter 1: Different Life Insurance Types..........................13

Chapter 2: Warning – Deceptive Sales Tactics...................19

Chapter 3: Best Type Policy For Most People....................29

Chapter 4: How Much Do You REALLY Need?.................37

Chapter 5: Beneficiary Designations...................................43

Chapter 6: Where Is The Best Place To Find It?................47

Chapter 7: Conclusion and Checklist 55

About the Author:...59

Other Books By Keith Maderer:..61

Your Opinion Matters:..62

Please Share on Social Media...63

Why I Wrote This Book

For 30 plus years I have helped clients find the lowest cost, best quality life insurance policies to protect their growing families in the event of death.

I have 5 adult children of my own and they are now getting married, buying houses, having babies (Yeah! Grandchildren) and building lives of their own.

I have been able to guide them through this process, avoiding the potholes and pitfalls that jumped in their way. But I am not your father... or your financial adviser.

I wrote this book because you... and every young couple, should be able to use my knowledge and experience to find the lowest cost, best life insurance policies to protect your family.

I will show you what to do each step of the way. I will give you small challenges that you can accomplish in minutes... then move on to the next.

Each challenge will bring you one step closer to the final goal.

Each challenge will teach you a lesson and help you find an answer to your own question.

Each challenge will help you save money, eliminate stress and find peace of mind.

This book is my way of giving back and helping young couples to navigate the maze of financial jargon and life insurance rhetoric.

Take this short journey and I guarantee you will learn some valuable lessons, save money, and make the best decisions for you and your family.

Who Should Read This Book

Did you just get married... or engaged?
Did you just buy your first house?
Did you, or your better half, just give birth to a beautiful bundle of joy... or maybe your 2nd?
Did you just start that new career after all those years in school?

If you answer "Yes" to 2 or more of these questions....
This book is for you.

You can blaze your own path in life. You can build a life for your family that will satisfy your needs and make you happy.

You are gaining confidence, building character and gaining responsibilities. With that, you know reality can be cruel at times.

Every day... 360,000 new babies are born... but 151,600 people also die every day.

That is over 105 people every minute... of every day.

I don't say this to scare you. It is a statistical fact of life and is based on research from the Population Reference Bureau.

If you are like most young couples, you can think of dozens, even hundreds of better things to do with your hard earned money... than spend it on life insurance.

The bottom line is you need life insurance to protect your lifestyle, your assets... and most importantly... your family.

Problem: Some of you rely on that immortality thing. You believe... *"I am immortal...."*

No... you aren't.

Problem: But life insurance sales people are so pushy... so slick... so Ew!... as Jimmy Fallon would say.

The good news is... **you are right**. Some are. You may even have a friend from high school or college that sells insurance. Maybe they are calling you to "Share some great ideas". You try to be nice, but they are persistent.

Problem: Doesn't it cost thousands of dollars?

It can, but if you know what to look for and where to find it, a few hundred dollars a year might be all you need to spend.

I will help you solve these problems and provide a simple, low-cost alternative. It will fit your budget and provide enough protection to handle your needs.

Don't wait until that friend from school is at your kitchen table pitching an expensive life insurance package. Read this book... take control... and check "**life Insurance**" off your to-do list.

Chapter 1: Different Life Insurance Types

First Challenge:

Your first challenge is to learn some of the basics about life insurance. After just a few short pages, you will know more about life insurance than 80% of the world population and even some life insurance agents that sell policies every day.

Life insurance policies come in many different forms. There is whole life, single pay life, universal life, variable life, level term and decreasing term life. How do you know which type is best suited for you and your family?

The purpose of life insurance is simple...

If you die, they pay your beneficiaries a check in the amount of your policy face value.

So why are there so many different types of policies to choose from?

The answer is simple... but most people don't care. They only want to find the best policy to meet their needs and save some money if possible.

For those that would like the answer, you will find them by analyzing these different policies while looking at the people and situations that are best suited for each type.

Whole Life:

Whole life insurance is permanent insurance that builds a cash value within the policy. This is the most expensive type of insurance and the policy's cash value earns interest on a tax-deferred basis.

If you need money, you can borrow against the accumulated cash value without being taxed. If you borrow against the cash value and do not pay it back, the outstanding loan amount will be deducted from the death benefit paid to your beneficiaries.

Whole life may be appropriate for small burial policies with a death benefit from $5,000 to $25,000.

Single Pay Life:

A single pay whole life policy is one where you make one payment up front and the insurance company gives you a death benefit for the remainder of your life. As an example, you are age 40 and you pay $9,000 upfront for a $25,000 death benefit policy. This is just a fictitious example. These policies consider a variety of factors before they can calculate how much the single premium payment will be.

Your age, gender, tobacco history, current prescription medications, family history and current medical condition will all have a bearing on how much or how little this policy costs.

Single pay life policies are best suited for specific needs. It may be providing a death benefit to a charity, providing a smaller tax-free benefit to a loved one or funding a small specific project upon your death.

Universal Life:

Universal life is a type of permanent life insurance policy that combines term insurance with a money market-type investment that pays a market interest rate of return. Most of these policies have a very low guaranteed interest rate, but the actual rate that they pay will vary based on current market interest rates.

This hybrid type of life insurance was very popular when it was introduced because interest rates were much higher in the 1980's and 1990's. With current interest rates on the low end, these policies have become less popular.

They are also much more expensive than the term policies that they try to emulate. They are sold under the premise of having a cash savings account along with a term policy, but if you are a disciplined saver/investor, you will be better suited elsewhere.

Variable Universal Life:

Variable life and variable universal life are also classified as permanent policies. Their main difference is they offer an investment fund tied to a stock or bond mutual-fund investment for the savings side of their accumulated cash values. As with any stock or bond investment, returns are not guaranteed and can decrease in value.

For most people, these policies are not a great option for your life insurance needs. If the markets were to decrease dramatically, your premiums to keep the policy in force potentially could increase beyond the originally stated rates... or your policy could lapse in coverage.

Annual Renewable Term Life:

A term policy is straight insurance with no investment component. You're buying life insurance coverage that lasts for a set period of time provided you pay the monthly or annual premium.

Annually-renewable term policies are purchased on a year-by-year basis. Your premiums will change each year, most likely go up as you get older and you do NOT need to re-qualify by showing evidence of good health in order to keep these policies.

Level Term Life:

Level term life insurance policies provide term coverage but lock in your premium rates for a fixed number of years. As an example, you could buy a 10, 15, 20 or 30 year level term policy. These policies will provide continual coverage for the length of years you select when you apply for the coverage.

Example, a 10 year level term policy would cost less than a 20 year level term policy because the insurance company is taking the risk for an additional 10 years at the same price.

You might ask, does the 20 year policy cost twice as much as the 10 year? Generally not.

Here is an actual example, for a 30 year old male, non-smoker in good health. A $500,000 policy would cost approximately the following amounts for each term period:

- **10 Year Level Term: $165 annually**
- **15 Year Level Term: $185 annually** *(an additional 12% more)*
- **20 Year Level Term: $245 annually** *(an additional 48% more)*
- **30 Year Level Term: $400 annually** *(an additional 142% more)*

These are actual rates from one of the highly reputable sources you will find in Chapter 5 of this book.

Term life is suitable for people that want to pay low premiums for large amounts of life insurance protection and lock those rates in for a specified period of time. There are very few bells and whistles with these policies, you are paying for basic life insurance protection with no cash accumulation, dividends or interest.

Decreasing Term Life:

Decreasing term life insurance is a type of annual renewable term life insurance that provides a death benefit that decreases at a predetermined rate over the life of the policy.

Premiums are usually constant throughout the contract, and reductions in policy payout typically occur either monthly or annually depending on the company and policy. Term lengths can range anywhere between 1 year and 30 years.

Typically these are used to protect a home mortgage, business loan or other outstanding loan that decreases every month that a payment is made.

It is relatively inexpensive because of its specific term length and automatically reducing death benefit.

Challenge and Summary:

Your Challenge: Of the many types listed in this chapter, which do you believe would be best suited to protect your life and the needs of your family?

Insurance Type:	Best for my family:
Whole Life	[ ] Best [ ] Possible [ ] Not Right
Single Payment Life	[ ] Best [ ] Possible [ ] Not Right
Universal Life	[ ] Best [ ] Possible [ ] Not Right
Variable Universal Life	[ ] Best [ ] Possible [ ] Not Right
Annual Renewable Term Life	[ ] Best [ ] Possible [ ] Not Right
Level Term Life	[ ] Best [ ] Possible [ ] Not Right
Reducing Term Life	[ ] Best [ ] Possible [ ] Not Right

As you can see, there are many different types of insurance policies and each has its own uses, pitfalls and cost structure.

But the good news for you is that if you don't find the answer yourself by the time we hit Chapter 3, I will give you the answer that I have found to be the best type for the vast majority of people.

Before we go there, lets take a look at the challenges that are posed by some of the deceptive sales tactics that you may run into. If you are not careful, knowledgeable and aware of what is going on, you could fall victim to these and end up with a headache, a bad policy and a much smaller wallet.

Chapter 2: Warning – Deceptive Sales Tactics

Second Challenge:

Your second challenge is to avoid being taken advantage of in this process. In this chapter, I will show you several of the commonly used tactics and how to avoid them.

While most insurance companies do not condone unethical behavior in any manner from their sales force, there have been many incidents where questionable and deceptive sales tactics have been reported over the years.

It is extremely hard for any company to monitor exactly what is said between their customers and their sales agents. There are many techniques and practices that seem to fall into the gray area between salesmanship and deception.

One of the best ways to avoid these issues is to be aware that they exist and then trust your instincts. While we cannot cover every possibility out there, the following are some of the most common.

If you find yourself involved in any of these scenarios, politely attempt to remove yourself from the discussion and look elsewhere.

Life Insurance is there to serve one purpose... If you die, it pays your beneficiaries a tax free check for the face value of your policy. If they are selling it as anything else, move on.

Tactic 1: Using Life insurance for Retirement or Education Savings:

If the salesperson is telling you that you can use this life insurance policy to save for retirement or your children's education, you could, but it is one of the worst and most costly ways to achieve those goals. They will usually try to use a universal life or a variable universal life policy for this purpose. They will show you hypothetical illustrations, variable premium levels and basically try to convince you that their policy is a good investment... along with life insurance.

You will be paying for the term insurance premium plus an additional amount that goes directly into your "Savings" or separate account. What they may fail to tell you is that there are other costs associated with these policies and their automatic monthly savings withdrawals from your bank account.

Just say no... do your retirement and education savings elsewhere and separate. They each have different objectives and should be managed separately.

Tactic 2: Higher Cost Insurance = Higher Commissions Paid:

You probably already guessed that most, if not all, life insurance salespeople are paid by commission. In most cases, these agents will earn high up front commissions with much lower rates on renewals over the years. Commissions for life insurance tend to be between 40-100% of the first year premium, then 1-2% for renewals, and after 3 years often go away entirely.

There is also different payouts based on the type of insurance they sell.

As an example, permanent policies like whole, universal and variable life insurance are more expensive and will pay them a higher percentage (70-80%) of the first year premium.

Term insurance which is less expensive will pay a much lower percentage (40-50%) of the first year premium.

Now if they are looking out for your best interest... the term insurance is probably the best avenue. But if they are looking out for themselves or their company, the more expensive policies will provide them a much higher income. Potential buyers... beware.

Tactic 3: The Double Team:

This tactic is used quite often when they are training new agents or just want to intimidate or impress a potential buyer. They will tell you that they wanted to make sure you received the best attention and Agent A is a specialist in one area or another.

In reality, they are tag teaming you in order to get you to sign on the dotted line today. They know if they can convince you to buy now rather than look it over, they believe they have a much better chance of getting the sale and earning a commission.

If they are upfront and tell you that Agent A will be your agent, but he or she is still in training and Agent B is their manager or training agent, then give them points for honesty, but still be wary of what they will try to sell.

If it is not the right type or amount of insurance, you should still walk away and look elsewhere. Remember I will show you what type and exactly where to find it in the following chapters. So you should be able to avoid this tag team tactic "tongue-twister" entirely.

Tactic 4: Paid Up Additions – Most Expensive:

If you already own a life insurance policy and you see that your dividends are being paid and then used to buy "Paid Up Additions". It is probably time to look for a different insurance policy, agent and company.

Paid Up Additional life insurance is them most expensive type of insurance you can buy. It is purchased in very small amounts and added to your policy by using the dividends that are paid back to you from the company.

They may try to make you believe that this is a great opportunity to keep up with inflation or build for your future, but in reality, they get a commission check every time it happens.

Don't be fooled and if you already own one of these policies, consider changing it.

Tactic 5: Policy Dividends Pay Your Premium:

Since we are talking about life insurance dividends. Did you ever wonder why they are not taxable? It is because they are not earned... they are a refund of the premium that you just paid the company.

They generally overcharge on these policies just in case their costs go up, if they do not, they pay it back to you as a dividend.

This also happens when you have a universal life or whole life policy that is building cash value. That cash value is on their books and they earn more on it than they are paying you. The more cash in your account, the less insurance death benefit they are on the hook for if you die. Then they can afford to give some of your money back.

Years ago, some agents were telling people that their dividends would eventually pay their premiums for them. Sure when you have enough cash value and very little life insurance, they could be making enough money on your cash value to pay for your premiums, but that was your money in the first place.

Watch out if you hear any talk about dividends and premiums. Many very strong and highly rated life insurance companies do not pay dividends. They just insure your life with none of these sales tactics, bells or whistles. In return, they offer lower premiums.

Tactic 6: Multiple Policies Increase Your Costs:

This is one of my least favorite tactics. There is this unwritten rule in the life insurance industry. While I totally <u>disagree</u> with it, I was surprised how prevalent this practice is. Here it is in one short sentence.

"Never replace an existing policy... add another one to it." - WRONG

What this means is if you currently have a policy, the sales representative's job is to convince you to add more insurance, but keep both policies. As an example, if you have an older $100,000 whole life policy costing $800/year, but now you need $500,000 of protection, they would suggest a new $400,000 universal life policy costing another $2,000/year.

Life Insurance... Who Needs It?

In my opinion and practice, it is normally best to replace the old policy and consolidate into one $500,000 policy. If you get the right type of insurance, it may actually cost less than the $100,000 policy alone and you have increased your protection by 5 times.

Question: Why don't they replace old policies with new ones?

Answers: Commissions, company profits and too much paperwork.

The commissions paid to the previous sales person would stop. Other agents would not want someone doing that to them, so they reciprocate... at your expense.

Many times it is the same company for the new policy as it was for the old policy. Older policies can be more profitable for the company.

Replacing a policy requires too much paperwork. In most states there is a strict legal process of full disclosure that must be followed before you can replace existing insurance. There is a waiting period while the original company is notified, which in turn prompts them to send out one of their policy conservation specialists to try to save the business and confuse or deter the customer from changing their policy.

For this reason many life insurance agents will not do what is in your best interest, because it jeopardizes their sale, their commission and it is more work for them. Wow... wonder who **they** are looking out for.

Years ago, I came a cross a local businessman that had 23 different life insurance policies from 5 different companies that he purchased (or was sold) over the last 20 years. Most were $5,000 and $10,000 whole life policies with one $50,000 term policy. He had a total of $210,000 of life insurance and he was paying over $4,000 annually.

This was the worst case I had ever seen. The bottom line was that he needed more protection. He ran a very successful business, had a wife, 4 children and some large college and wedding expenses in the near future.

We replaced all 23 policies with one $750,000 policy and his cost was only $1,300 per year. We took all the cash value from his previous policies and placed it in an account for the upcoming college and wedding expenses. We also added the $2,700+ each year that he was saving on his insurance. That action was in the client's best interest. It took a lot of paperwork, time and effort, but it was the right thing to do.

Keep this in mind as you maneuver through the potential obstacles that are trying to take advantage of your hard earned money.

Tactic 7: Extra Riders = Extra Cost = Extra Commissions Paid:
There are many riders that you can add to your life insurance policies. Some are reasonable and a good value, others are not worth the additional cost. Every time you add a rider, your monthly or annual premium will increase as well. This means that the sales person's commission will go up too. You need to understand your needs and what riders would fit the best to help you meet them.

1. Waiver of Premium: This rider will pay your premiums for you if you become disabled. It is usually worth the extra cost and adds safety to your policy. **YES**
2. Spousal Rider: This one will allow you to purchase a certain amount of protection on your spouse for a specified cost depending on their age, gender and health. In some cases this is worth it, but in most it is better to take a separate policy. **MAYBE**
3. Children's Insurance Rider: As it says, this allows you to purchase protection on your children. It usually comes in units of $5,000, $10,000, etc. and is very reasonably priced. The best part is that one price covers any and all of your naturally born or legally adopted children. If you eventually have 5 children, it cost the same as if you only had 1 child. There are some additional benefits to this rider, but this is a keeper. As soon as you have your first child, add it to one of the policies. I normally add it to the wife's policy as women live longer and have lower premiums. **YES**
4. Accidental Death and Dismemberment Rider: This rider will

pay your family double if you die or loose a limb in an accident. While it is a fairly inexpensive rider, I don't recommend it for 2 reasons. First if you have the right amount of insurance to start with, why do you need to double it.

Second, it is much harder to collect this double indemnity because the insurance companies will try to find every reason not to pay. They will look for any loophole or other medical reason to disqualify your claim. As an example. You are in a car accident, then taken to the hospital and die 72 hours later. They might contend that you were alive after the accident and died due to complications in the hospital... claim denied. Insurance journals have these types of examples everywhere. You may need to hire a lawyer to get this paid and by the time it is all said and done, it may cost more than it is worth. This one is a **NO**.

5. <u>Other Riders:</u> there are many other riders that you can consider, but the ones above are the most commonly used. Some of these include: Disability income, Return of premium, Accelerated death benefit, Critical illness, Term conversion and Guaranteed insurability riders. Most of these are used in special situations and if you think they might be relevant, you can Google them for more information.

Other Guilt Related Sales Tactics:

Careers in sales can be very profitable for the right individuals. If you have a great product or service, you should not need to use questionable or unethical sales practices to motivate potential buyers.

But there are some sales people that have less integrity and choose to use whatever methods they can to convince prospects to make a purchase. Here are some guilt related tactics that I have been told about by clients of mine over the years.

What if you die or are in an accident tomorrow? Then it will be too late.

Who will take care of your family if you are gone? The State or Federal government.

Don't you want to take care of your spouse and children? What are you a monster?

Your health is good right now... but tomorrow it could change.

This is a great deal from a great company... don't be stupid... just sign here.

While these may be true statements, if they are used in a way to embarrass or guilt you into buying on the spot, they are pressure tactics to avoid.

Hard to believe that you would need to guilt someone into purchasing something that they need, but these tactics and many more are being used everyday.

Don't fall victim to it. Trust your instincts. If you feel that you are being pressured, walk away. If it is as good as they say it is, it will be there tomorrow or next week.

Challenge and Summary:

Your Challenge: Identify whether you or anyone you know has been exposed to any of these deceptive sales tactics. Now that you are aware of their existence and purpose, you should be able to identify if you have ever been exposed to any of them or if a family member or friend has ever been a target.

Deceptive Sales Tactics	Your Exposure		
Retirement or Education Savings?	[ ] I have been	[ ] Family or Friend	[ ] None
Higher Cost = More Commission	[ ] I have been	[ ] Family or Friend	[ ] None
The Double Team	[ ] I have been	[ ] Family or Friend	[ ] None
Paid Up Additions	[ ] I have been	[ ] Family or Friend	[ ] None

Let Dividends Pay Premiums	[ ] I have been	[ ] Family or Friend	[ ] None
Multiple Policies	[ ] I have been	[ ] Family or Friend	[ ] None
Extra Riders – Extra Commission	[ ] I have been	[ ] Family or Friend	[ ] None
Guilt Tactics	[ ] I have been	[ ] Family or Friend	[ ] None

While the vast majority of insurance agents are very nice, personable and ethical people working for highly rated and quality insurance companies, there are others that can give the entire industry a bad reputation.

It is hard to believe that I had to dedicate a whole chapter to warn you about the many deceptive sales tactics out there. But if you are not careful, you can and will be taken advantage of. These less than ethical individuals know how much money they can make by selling life insurance and are only looking out for themselves.

While their actions don't physically hurt you. It could be a costly mistake and take some time, effort and expense to correct their mess after it is in place.

If you find that you already have a life insurance mess, don't stress over it. Just take the proactive steps in this book to correct it... and move on with your life.

The remainder of this book will show you the right way to do it. It is not hard, but you can, and should fix it. Every dollar that you are spending in excess of what you should be spending is a waste. A waste of your time... a waste of your money... and a waste of your potential future opportunities.

The money you save by doing it right can help fund a family vacation, education, retirement savings and many other goals.

You deserve the best... now let me help you find it.

Chapter 3: Best Type Policy For Most People

Third Challenge:

Your third challenge is to find the best type of policy to suit your needs and the needs of your family. Once you know this, you can then proceed to figure out the amount you need, where to get it, and how to structure the policy to fit your personal situation.

Have you already figured out which type of life insurance I believe is best suited for the vast majority of people?

My educated bias is based on personal experience and watching the evolution of the insurance industry over the past 35+ years. I have seen new policies introduced and existing policies improved or modified. Mortality rates and premium costs have declined multiple times due to medical advancements that are keeping us alive longer... and healthier.

Will this continue in the future? My guess is that it will, and with that, the improvements that will be made to the life insurance industry should make future policies even more competitive and less costly moving forward.

WARNING: But don't procrastinate thinking that the longer you wait, the better rates will be. With that mindset, you will be waiting until it doesn't matter anymore... because you will be dead.

Take advantage of the current rates and know that by selecting the policies that I will talk about below, you will have paid the least amount for the most coverage and your family will be protected in the event that something bad happens.

So which type of policy do I personally own and recommend? Here it is.

Level Term:

As I have said before, the primary purpose of life insurance is to protect your family by providing a large tax-free cash infusion upon your premature death. Not save for college or retirement. Not

Life Insurance... Who Needs It?

double the amount if you die in an accident. Not pay you if you become disabled.

If you die prematurely, it is there to make sure that your family receives a large enough check to live comfortably. It allows you to take care of your children's education and live out the rest of their lives in the fashion that you would have wanted them to... if you were still alive.

The best life insurance type to handle this need is the Level Term Life policy. This is because it only provides life insurance. No cash value, no dividends, no bells, no whistles. Just straight up protection if you pass away before you have lived a long and prosperous life.

It also provides the protection at the lowest possible cost to you. So you can get the biggest bang for your buck and stay within your monthly budget at the same time.

How To Select Your Term:

The next question that you may be asking is... What term should I select?

This takes a little thought, but even if you get it wrong, the good news is that you will not be penalized financially if you figure it out later and try to correct it. Providing you do it fairly soon and your health hasn't deteriorated dramatically in the process.

Term policies come in all sizes. There is annually renewable, 5 year, 10, 15, 20, 25 and now 30 year term policies. Each one is based on the time frame that the insurance company will be taking the risk of protecting your financial life.

So it makes sense that the 1 year term will cost less than the 5 year, but it will increase every year. The 10 year is less than the 30 year, but their rates are locked in for the duration of their term.

The insurance company, with the help of Actuarial accounting, is trying to predict how long you will live, then protect your life at the lowest possible cost and still make a profit. The insurance industry is becoming more an more competitive as the internet allows for better and faster information.

So how do you select your term?

First you look at what needs you are trying to protect. If you have young children, you may want to make sure that their college education is protected. For a newborn, that is about 20 years. Do you have a mortgage on your house? How many years remain? 15 to 30 are the most common.

Next you have to look at the way these needs get paid for. Every year you live, you are paying your mortgage payment, providing living expenses for your family and hopefully savings for your children's education and your own retirement.

So each of these needs is decreasing every day, every month, every year that you live. By selecting a term that covers most of your need and allows you time to build assets in the event that you live, this is the best term for you.

In most cases I recommend a 20 year level term policy if you are under age 40. The older you get , the shorter the term you should need if you have been saving and accumulating assets to help meet your longer term goals.

By selecting the 20 year level term policy you will get great low rates and lock them in for 20 years. During these 20 years you now have peace of mind and plenty of time to plan for the rest of your financial future.

Select Your Riders Wisely:

For most young families, there are 2-3 riders that you will want to add to your policy. As mentioned in the previous chapter, Waiver of Premium, Children's Insurance Rider and possibly a Spousal Rider are the main three that you will want to consider.

Remember that each of these riders will cost additional dollars, so weighing the benefits versus the additional cost is an important factor.

Why do you need Waiver of Premium?

This rider is relatively inexpensive and will pay your premiums for you if you become seriously ill or disabled. It will only pay the cost of the insurance, but for a term policy that is the entire premium. If you are seriously ill or unable to work, you can apply to have this waiver activated. Medical evidence is needed from your attending physician, but in most legitimate cases this will be easy enough to prove.

Why do you need a Children's Insurance Rider?

A children's rider can be the least expensive way to provide a basic layer of life insurance protection on each and every child in your family. These riders are normally purchased in units of $5,000 and can go as high as $25,000. This rider provides a death benefit in case a child dies before a specified age which is normally age 25. After the child reaches the age of maturity (between ages 18 to 25 form most policies), this term rider can be converted into permanent insurance coverage up to five times the original face amount without the need for medical exams or evidence of insurability.

This rider provides protection for one and all children in your family at the exact same cost per family... not per child. One child cost the exact same as it does for 5, 7 or even 10 children.

PLEASE NOTE:

This rider will provide coverage in the event your child dies from any reason before the term expires. It will also provide future protection at guaranteed rates in the event that your child is diagnosed with any health issues, life threatening medical conditions or any other condition that would cause them to be denied or rated for insurance in the future. You do need to exercise this future purchase option before the age that the policy no longer covers that child.

Why might you want to add a Spousal Rider?

Depending on the age and health of your spouse, it might be less expensive to add them to your policy with a spousal rider. Normally you cannot add them for a death benefit more than yours, but some companies do allow this.

In many cases it is easier and less costly to take a separate policy for your spouse. This is usually the case if you are looking for a reasonably large amount of life insurance ($500,000 or more) on each spouse because both are working and making close to the same amount of income annually.

Riders do matter and they can make a good policy... even better. Just be sure to select them wisely.

The End of The Term:

The big question.... what happens to your insurance at the end of your term?

Correct... it expires.

But you have options. If you have a 20 year level term policy, I suggest that you revisit that policy every 5 years, just to make sure that it still covers your anticipated needs. If your life, income or family has changed dramatically, you may need to reassess your needs and make changes.

If that is the case, you have 15 years of coverage left, but you may want to apply for an entirely new Life insurance policy which may or may not be with the same company. You may need more... or less coverage. You may want a longer... or shorter term. Whatever it is, you can reapply for the new policy and wait for the results. If everything comes back approved as expected, you can then just cancel the other policy and stop making payments.

IMPORTANT Note:

Never cancel, stop paying for, or surrender your existing policy until you have a new one in place and paid for. It is better to pay for an extra month or two and have double the coverage, than to have no coverage and something bad happens. Enough said.

Challenge and Summary:

Your Challenge: With your knowledge about level term policies, list the advantages that would be most applicable to your own situation.

Policy Features:	Needed:	May Be Needed:	Not Important:
Lower Premium Cost	[ ]	[ ]	[ ]
Flexible Term in Years	[ ]	[ ]	[ ]
Level Fixed Premiums	[ ]	[ ]	[ ]
Multiple Riders	[ ]	[ ]	[ ]
Simple Policy Structure	[ ]	[ ]	[ ]
Easy to Change/Update	[ ]	[ ]	[ ]

I have helped many people afford coverage that meets or slightly exceeds their needs. In many cases, this means hundreds or thousands or even millions of dollars of life insurance protection. If they had to pay for whole life or universal life, the annual cost would be astronomical and would most likely place a big strain on their family budget.

Level term allows us to make sure that your family receives a big enough tax-free check to invest and live comfortably for the rest of their lives in the event of your premature death. It allows you to add only the riders you need and structure your premium payments on a monthly, quarterly, semi-annual or annual basis... whichever best fits your cash flow and budget.

It also allows the flexibility to cancel your policy if your needs change or if you purchase a new policy *(before getting rid of the existing one)* that better fits your situation and possibly at a lower cost. You won't have to worry about cash values, 1035 exchanges, potential dividends or rollovers.

You just stop paying the premiums... and your insurance is canceled.

Congratulations! You are now ready to figure out how much you need.

Chapter 4: How Much Do You REALLY Need?

Fourth Challenge:

Your fourth challenge is to determine the correct amount of insurance that will properly protect your family if you or your spouse die prematurely. Don't let this part intimidate you. You have armed yourself with the knowledge of the last few chapters and this will continue your education and answer a very big piece of your life insurance puzzle.

In this chapter we will look at several methods for calculating your needs. I will also share some thoughts about break points, the renewal process and the reality of how your life insurance needs change over time.

I have hand selected multiple sources for you to use that have no conflict of interest. By that I mean that these online resources are not tied directly to any specific insurance companies which could make them skew their calculations toward making sales for their company. They are all independently provided for your use and benefit.

While their methods, numbers and results may differ slightly, if you use one or two to get your calculations, you should find your desired range. Then we can look at insurance company breakpoints to fine tune your selection and purchase decisions. Let's get started.

Online Resources:

The internet is a great place to look for answers. I have included several sites that provide free - life insurance needs calculators to help you with this process. It will take about 5-10 minutes with each of these to figure out your need, but it will be time well spent. I recommend that you try 2-3 of them and compare your results. They all have a tendency to calculate a little higher need than the more advanced method that I use (Cash Flow Analysis - below), but they do give you a reasonable basis for making your decision without a lot of time spent on inputting information.

BankRate.com:

http://www.bankrate.com/calculators/insurance/life-insurance-calculator.aspx

YahooFinance.com:

http://finance.yahoo.com/calculator/insurance/ins01/?bypass=true

LifeHappens.org:

http://www.lifehappens.org/insurance-overview/life-insurance/calculate-your-needs/

CalcXML.com:

https://www.calcxml.com/calculators/life-insurance-calculator

Cash Flow Analysis:

This is the method that I use with my clients, it is much more detail oriented and takes your own personal cash flow, income, expenses and savings into consideration. We delve into your actual spending habits and then apply a factor to each cash flow item that represents what would happen if you passed away or if your spouse passes away.

By utilizing these figures we can accurately apply inflation, taxes and the present value formulas to your desired cash flow projections. We use a sophisticated computer program to do all the end result calculations, which in turn provides the present value of your actual insurance needs.

For those that live in our neck of the woods, the Western New York – Buffalo | Niagara region, you can contact me for more information if you would like to explore this further. For others, the online calculation method is a quick, fairly accurate alternative.

Break Points:

With reference to life insurance... what are break points?

A break point is when an insurance company sets its premium rates at a discount based on volume, face value or death benefit of the policy. Here are a few examples:

A $100,000 policy would cost less than a $95,000 policy because there is a break point at $100,000. A $1,000,000 policy would cost less than a $960,000 policy at some companies because $1 million is a break point. You can see where I am going with this.

Here are some of the most significant break points.

$100,000 - $250,000 - $500,000 - $1,000,000 - $1,500,000 - $2,000,000 and so forth.

So how can you use this information to save money?

If your calculated insurance need is $1,467,590, it might actually cost less to apply for a $1,500,000 life insurance policy. When you hit the next chapter, you can actually compare the costs of both policy amounts and make a decision based on the results.

For the purpose of this chapter, you just need to be aware that breakpoints could save you precious dollars and provide slightly more coverage for less cost.

Renewal Process:

So what happens at the end of your 10 or 20 year term? What if you still need insurance, just a different type, term or amount?

Important Note: You should begin looking into this 6-12 months before your term expires.

First, recalculate your needs and take a look at the options that are available. You can then approach your existing insurer and ask for a quote and if they would require any evidence of insurability.

Second, check a couple of the resources in the next chapter and get their best quote and compare the offers.

Select the best one and apply for the new insurance as needed.

Insurance Needs Over Time:

Every year that you live... you are providing income to cover the living expenses, savings and investments of your family.

Every year you live... your mortgage reduces, your car and student loans are paid down and your life insurance needs will decrease.

Every year you live... we hope your savings and investments are increasing in value. Your retirement, 401K and property values are increasing... which will also reduce your overall need for life insurance.

So why do I bring this up? Every year you live should be an opportunity to make your net worth grow. To increase your assets, reduce your liabilities and build a safer and less risky future for your family.

This should continue to make your life insurance needs decline and your net worth grow as you get older. The chart below is a very simple way of looking at this concept. Obviously, the uniformity of this chart is never the same for any 2 families. Your numbers can be similar or completely different.

Life Insurance... Who Needs It?

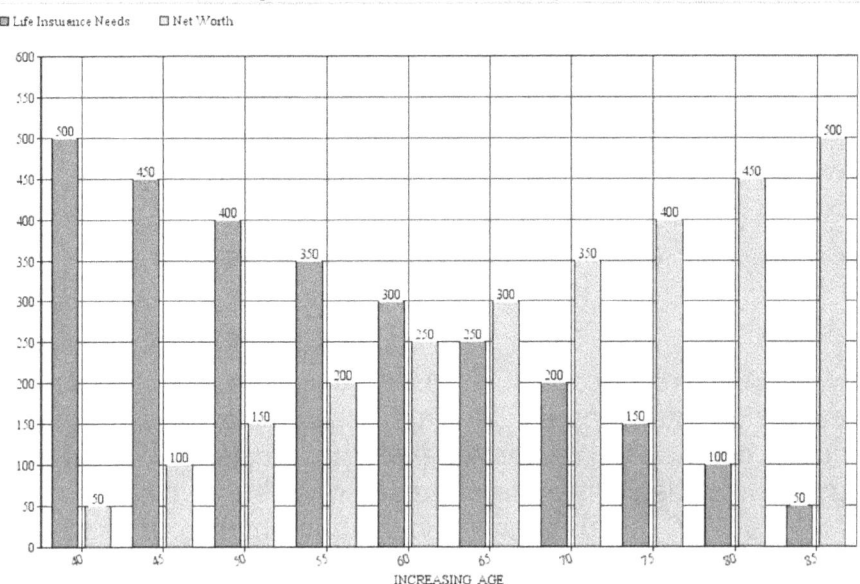

The idea is that you need to consider this, and at some age in the future... you may have accumulated a large enough net worth to match or surpass your life insurance needs.

From this point on, you no longer need life insurance. In the chart above, it is somewhere between ages 60 and 65. Your numbers will be unique to your family and your financial success.

Challenge and Summary:

Your Challenge: From the resources provided in this chapter, determine your current insurance need, your spouses and any riders that you feel you need to add to the policy.

Online Resource	Your Need	Spouse's Need	Child Rider	Other Riders
Resource 1	$	$	[ ] Yes __ $5,000 Units	[ ] Waiver of premium

Resource 2	$	$	[ ] Yes ___ $5,000 Units	[ ] Waiver of premium
Resource 3	$	$	[ ] Yes ___ $5,000 Units	[ ] Waiver of premium
Totals:	$	$		
Average Need:	$	$		
Closest Break Point	$	$		

Now you have successfully used the free, unbiased online resources or your own cash flow analysis to determine your family's life insurance needs. You have taken these calculations, averaged them and rounded off to the nearest higher break point or nearest $10,000 to $100,000 depending on the amount of your needs.

Now we need to take a look at how to structure your beneficiary designations so that you avoid future problems and make sure that your proceeds will be distributed tax free to your beneficiaries.

Chapter 5: Beneficiary Designations

Fifth Challenge:

Your fifth challenge is properly structure your beneficiary designations. This will be a very easy challenge to complete, but you do need to read this brief chapter to avoid some common mistakes and do it properly.

Supersede Your Will:

Most people are not aware of the fact that a life insurance policy is a contract between you and the company. The provisions of this contract will supersede the provisions of your Last Will and Testament if done properly.

Why would you want that to happen?

If you allow the proceeds of your life insurance to be funneled through your will, and then disbursed to your beneficiaries, they can become subject to probate and administration expenses. This could delay your family from being able to use these proceeds by months. This could also cost an additional 5% or more to be paid to attorneys, court costs and other estate shrinkage factors.

The good news is that you can avoid all of that by following the guidelines below.

As Per Owners Estate:

First lets look at what **NOT** to do...

Do **NOT** use these words in any of your beneficiary designations. If you use these words as your beneficiary designation, the beneficiary automatically reverts back to your Last Will and Testament. Which is exactly what you are trying to avoid. For many years, I witnessed life insurance agents and some lawyers recommend that you use "As Per Owners Estate" as their primary beneficiary designation.

Why would they do that?

Life insurance agents can be lazy. Instead of filling out all the details about who, what and how you want your beneficiaries set up, it was easier to just write... As Per Owners Estate. Don't let laziness cost your family thousands or even tens of thousands of dollars. Make them do their job and help fill out the form completely.

Some Lawyers suggest that you use this as well. Their reasons are different. If you have a million dollar life insurance policy that now has to go through your estate, probate and administration... they stand to make 5% of that amount to handle the paperwork... that is $50,000.

That is a lot of money that your family will never see if you allow this to happen. You just need to file a few short claim forms and provide a death certificate... it is a very simple and straight forward process. Definitely not worth paying $50,000 for.

Specific Names and Numbers:

Every insurance company has their own designated beneficiary forms. On your original application, there is also a section to fill out these designations. There is a section for Primary Beneficiaries and another for Contingent Beneficiaries. They usually have 2 - 4 sections on each to fill in the name, address, date of birth, relationship to you, tax ID number and percentage of the total that you would like this individual, organization or charity to receive.

For most families, your spouse would be your Primary Beneficiary at 100%. If you have children, they would be your Contingent Beneficiary, divided equally between all of them and any future children that are born or legally adopted. If you detail these items out as specifically as possible then the insurance company can handle the entire administration of your insurance proceeds... saving your family a large amount of time, headache and money.

What if I need more room because I have 6 children?

You can attach a separate statement that outlines all of the information that the insurance company requires and attach it to the form. You will need to write "See Attached Statement" in the

Life Insurance... Who Needs It?

appropriate section on the original form. Your statement would also be signed, dated and if necessary notarized.

Challenge and Summary:

Your Challenge: While naming your beneficiaries can be a very simple item, it is very important to make sure that you fill them out accurately and completely. Don't rush through this short challenge or it could cost your loved ones dearly. Use the chart below to map out your wishes and complete the forms.

Your Primary Beneficiary Designations

Name:	Date of Birth:	Address:	Relationship:	Percentage:

Your Contingent Beneficiary Designations

Name:	Date of Birth:	Address:	Relationship:	Percentage:

For a more in depth discussion and even more ways to use

beneficiary designations to handle and simplify your estate - Check the **Simple Problem Solvers** book on my Amazon Author Page – http://amazon.com/author/keithmaderer

Congratulations... You are now ready to research and compare companies, terms and policies to find the lowest cost, highest rated and most suitable life insurance to meet your needs. Then submit an application and start the process.

Chapter 6: Where Is The Best Place To Find It?

Sixth Challenge:

Your sixth challenge is to take the information that you have already gathered and calculated about your life insurance types, needs, beneficiaries and specific amounts... and find the best deal.

Find the best rated and lowest cost company to contact, fill out an application, provide the necessary medical information and get your life insurance policy underwritten and in force.

That sounds like a hefty challenge... but you are going to find that it is much easier than you think. It may take a few weeks to a couple months for the entire process, but most of the work is done by the insurance company on your behalf.

Let's get started...

Online Resources:

There are many ways to find great information about life insurance policies, rates and riders. You could Google - Term Life Insurance Rates and you would be offered plenty of company specific websites that would allow you to take a look at their company policies.

But over the past 15 years, a new type of site has been gaining popularity. These sites will compare insurance companies, their policies and premiums for you and provide a listing of the top insurers with the lowest premiums to meet your specifications. They have already done the heavy lifting for you. Just type in some basic information and click - Compare Rates.

Here are some of the sites that I recommend using. I prefer these sites because to the best of my knowledge, they have no direct ties to any of the insurance companies that they compare. They are unbiased and will help you apply to any of the listed companies that you prefer.

Term4Sale.com:	https://www.term4sale.com/
LifeQuotes.com:	http://www.lifequotes.com/
Intelliquote.com:	https://www.intelliquote.com/
AccuQuote.com:	https://www.accuquote.com/home-3/
InstantQuote.com:	https://www.instantquotelifeinsurance.com/
QuickQuote.com:	https://www.quickquote.com/

Check them out and give them a test drive. Fill in the blanks and see what type of rates you find. When you are satisfied that you have narrowed down your choices, hit the – Apply Button. This will start the application process.

Step By Step Process:

Now lets take a look at what will happen when you find the insurance quote and click the – APPLY Button.

First: A screen will come up asking for your name, email and phone number. It may also request your address and a few simple health questions. That depends on the site and the state.

Second: You will receive an email after you submit this information confirming your application inquiry.

Third: You should receive a phone call within 24 - 48 hours from a licensed insurance agent that will walk you through the application process and guidelines.

Fourth: This person will either schedule an appointment at your house or a local medical office to have a nurse complete the medical questionnaire and some basic testing. This basic testing will most likely include a urine test, a blood test, blood pressure readings, height and weight.

Fifth: All of this information will be submitted to your selected company and will be given to their underwriting team for review.

Sixth: Sit back and wait for the results.

Medical Information:

Over the years I have helped many individuals and families to acquire the best life insurance to meet their needs. One of the most common concerns that they have is their health. Some think they should wait until they "get back in shape" or "until I lose that extra 10 pounds" or "once I quit smoking".

While these are all great things to strive for... they are already recorded in your medical records. When you apply for life insurance, you are allowing the insurance company to perform their own medical testing and to access your existing medical records through the Medical Information Bureau or MIB. This is a confidential service that all medical professionals are obligated to update with your current medical information.

CAUTION: If you are considering making a false statement on your life insurance application, it will be caught if that answer does not match the one on the MIB.

If you say you never smoked cigarettes or were never treated for diabetes or any other previously diagnosed conditions, but your medical records indicate otherwise... your policy will probably be denied or at best severely rated to a higher premium cost.

Don't play games with the underwriting process. Just answer the questions to the best of your ability and allow the underwriters to do their job. What I have found over the years is that something you think is really bad, is more common and less life threatening to an underwriter.

They are looking at "Insurance" medicine versus your personal physician looking at life medicine. They often have substantially different objectives.

Policy Approval or Alternate Offer Process:

You have applied, taken your medical exam, answered your questionnaire and the underwriters are doing their job. What can you expect next?

Best Scenario:

Ideally, your health is good and everything will be approved as applied for. This process will usually take between 2 weeks to 2 months. Then all you need to do is make your first payment and your policy is in force.

Common Scenario:

But in about 20% of the cases, the underwriter finds something in your medical history or the current tests that would cause them to deny your approval as you requested it. For these individuals, an alternate offer will be made. In most cases that means that for a slightly higher cost or a different rating class, they will approve the insurance. You will need to accept this higher premium and these conditions, or you can walk away and try another company.

Over the years, I have found that the underwriting process at most insurance companies are pretty similar. If one company offers you a rated or higher premium, the others will probably do the same. You can attempt to go through the entire process again, but chances are you end up with a similar or even worse outcome. Not to mention the loss of time by repeating the process.

Why would it be a worse outcome? If you have already selected the best, lowest cost company to meet your needs, the second best probably cost more to start with. So when they do their underwriting, chances are pretty good that their offer, will be slightly more expensive than your first choice company's offer.

If this happens in your case... take a deep breath and let them know you need a few days to think about it. Talk it over with your family and listen to their input.

Personally... I would accept the policy. Pay the new premium. Start it on a monthly or quarterly basis and then if you want to try another company to see if you can do better... do it. Now you have protection. As long as you pay your premiums, you are covered.

If you find a better deal later, you can always stop paying the first policy, cancel it and move on. But remember this is not highly likely, but could happen.

Worst Case Scenario:

In a very small percentage of applications, they company will deny your application outright without any alternate offer. This is usually due to a much more serious medical issue or possibly a fraudulent response on your application.

Most people that this happens to, are aware of the issue and were either trying to hide it, or were hoping they could get insured anyway.

Unfortunately, these individuals may have a hard time getting life insurance anywhere at a reasonable cost. They may have to buy guaranteed life insurance which usually has a very low benefit, a high premium and a lot of disqualification restrictions. But this book is not written for that extreme minority of situations.

Constructive Receipt and Acceptance:

Now that you have completed the underwriting process and your policy is approved, you need to take the final step to get your coverage and protection in force.

If you have not already made a premium payment, you need to do this first before your policy can be considered a legal binding contract. Once the insurance company approves your policy and accepts your payment, you are now legally covered.

You should also have constructive receipt of the actual physical policy and returned some sort of acknowledgment that you have received it. Your constructive receipt is important because it tells the insurance company that you have received, reviewed and accepted the policy as it is written. This is especially important if there were changes to your originally requested coverage or premium ratings.

Be sure to review the policy cover page and riders that are attached. You should also find a copy of your original application and medical questionnaires attached in the back of the policy. If everything meets your approval... sign the receipt and return with your payment. If not... ask questions.

Challenge and Summary:

Your Challenge: In this chapter, we have challenged you to take your calculated needs and begin investigating the best companies with the lowest cost structure and actually applying for your new policy. Complete this checklist and fill in the blanks for dates and actions.

Actions Taken:	Your – Date Completed	Spouse's – Date completed
Online Selection Screening	___/___/_____	___/___/_____
Application Submitted	___/___/_____	___/___/_____
Medical Info. Completed	___/___/_____	___/___/_____
Approval or Offer Received	___/___/_____	___/___/_____
Premium Payment Made	___/___/_____	___/___/_____
Receipt and Acceptance	___/___/_____	___/___/_____

You have now purchased the best quality, lowest cost life insurance policy that meets your family's needs. You helped your family protect against the uncertainties that can and do arise in real life.

You also saved your family hundreds if not thousands of dollars each year.

Congratulations! You deserve a reward. Take your family out to dinner and a movie.. or on a day trip to your favorite spot. You made a smart decision and now it is time to relax and enjoy!

Chapter 7: Conclusion and Checklist

Seventh Challenge:

Your final challenge is to go back and complete any of the previous challenges that you have not yet started. Many people, including myself, like to read the entire book first to gather the information and then re-read and take each step, one at a time.

If this is your intention, you now know exactly what to do in order to complete this challenge. The sooner you start, the sooner you can move on.

I will recap the main steps that you have learned and should follow. I will also offer a few more insights and wisdom that you should consider as you navigate through the years.

Select The Correct Type:

Chapter one gave you the ammunition and knowledge to differentiate between the various type of life insurance that you my come across. It also highlighted pros and cons of these different types along with some situations where they are used.

Avoid Pitfalls and Deception:

Chapter two offered a warning and a brief outline of some of the most common pitfalls and deceptive tactics that are being used out in the real world. Your knowledge of these tactics will help you steer clear and avoid being taken advantage of by less than ethical sales people.

If you find that you have already fallen victim to one of these deceptions, you now have the power and education to be able to fix it, move on and make significantly better decisions moving forward. The money you will save can help with retirement, education or just taking a great family vacation.

My Personal Recommendation:

Chapter 3 spelled out what I believe is the best type of insurance for the vast majority of people. It also helped determine the correct term, riders and other options that you can take advantage of in order to provide the best protection at the most reasonable cost for your family.

Pick A Number:

In Chapter 4, I provided multiple resources to help you determine just how much life insurance you really need to protect your family in the event of your premature death. We discussed the use of Break Points, cash flow analysis and how the insurance renewal process can be efficiently managed.

I also shared a chart that offers a visual representation of how your life insurance needs and personal net worth work in opposite directions. This illustration will show how you can design your future to eventually eliminate your need for life insurance and live a very comfortable life for you and your family.

Who To Leave It To:

In Chapter 5 we took a break and discussed the importance of properly drafting your beneficiary designations. This short challenge is one that could save tens of thousands of dollars for your family if done right... or cost them the same if done wrong.

Please don't take this one lightly. Spend time to read and review this information before you finalize your insurance application.

If you happen to read this chapter and realize that you may have done something wrong with your 401K, IRA or any other beneficiary designations, you now know how to fix it. Contact the company, request their form and fill it out the right way. It doesn't get much easier than that.

Get It Here:

In Chapter 6 you get to have some fun. The online resources that are provided will offer you plenty of ways to find great companies, policies and most importantly... the lowest rates available. By using these services, you can reduce your time and research by weeks.

I then take you by the hand and explain what to expect each step along the way. Your efforts here will pay huge rewards to your bottom line. The savings that you accumulate could be the difference that allows you and your family to prosper and build a very sizable estate. It could help you to retire early or make sure your kids get a great education. It could just help you to enjoy life more and spend more time with your loved ones.

Whatever you choose to do with your savings, it should provide peace of mind that you made a wise decision and didn't allow yourself or your family to be taken advantage of.

Regular Review:

One final piece of advice. As with anything in life, life insurance needs to be reviewed and updated if something changes. Any time there is a major life event, take some time afterwards to review your needs, plans and objectives.

Major life events include the following:

Births, marriages, divorce, disability, death, retirement, unemployment, job changes, medical or health conditions, winning the lottery, starting a business, getting a promotion, buying or building a new house, needing assisted living or a nursing home.

Keep these in the back of your mind and make sure that you pull out those policies, wills, powers of attorney and other important documents if any of these situations arise.

It is better to review and realize everything is good, than to wait and find out it was not.

Congratulations:

You have finished your last challenge. It is my sincere hope that you enjoyed this book and the resources within. Please share these concepts with your parents, children, friends and co-workers. Your sharing may help them avoid headaches, pitfalls or correct mistakes that they have made due to real world deceptions.

I have shared these ideas and experience with you so you can make a better life for your family. Pay it forward and do the same for someone that you love or care about. They will thank you and you will have peace of mind that you helped someone else.

If you would like to thank me, have a question or suggestion about this book, I can be reached by email at keith@keithmaderer.com. I look forward to hearing from you.

Thank you for taking the time to challenge yourself, follow these steps and succeed in the life insurance arena. It is one of the most abused and misunderstood areas of personal finance.

P.S.

If you feel so inclined, I would be honored if you would write an honest book review on Amazon.com or Goodreads.com to help me learn what areas I can improve my writing and content.

About the Author:

Keith Maderer is an author, a dynamic and humorous speaker, an entrepreneur and a 30+ year veteran of the financial services industry. He completed the Certified Financial Planner (CFP) program in 1990 and has been a Fee-Only Registered Investment Adviser operating in Orchard Park, NY which is a suburb in the Buffalo/Niagara Falls region - since 1989. He works with individuals, pension plans and trusts to help them make simpler and better financial decisions.

He has been married to his high school sweetheart (Lori) for over 30 years (I hear she is up for sainthood) and has 5 adult children and 1 grandchild. He has been active in many local non-profit organizations and has served as a coach, League Commissioner and President of the Orchard Park Little League baseball program. He was the co-founder, President and team coach of the Orchard Park Youth Basketball Association and was the founder and managing director of the Maderer Foundation.

He actively volunteers in the District 65 Toastmasters International organization where he has served as President of both the Clarence Toastmasters and Larkin Leaders Toastmaster groups. He has achieved their highest designation of excellence in public speaking and leadership – the DTM (Distinguished Toastmaster Award) after only 4 years in the program.

He was the recipient of the Toastmaster's District 65 – Division A – Club President of the Year award in 2014 and the District 65 - Area Governor of the Year award in 2015. He was the first runner up in the District 65 International Speech Contest in 2016 and loves sharing stories, anecdotes and messages that help motivate and inspire others to achieve their own success.

His hobbies include Reading, Biking, Hiking, Photography, Golf,

Disc Golf and playing with his grandchildren.

For more information about Keith Maderer or to sign up for his **VIP email list**, please visit his website at KeithMaderer.com

When you sign up for the **VIP email list**, you will receive first notification of future book launches and special offers exclusively for insiders. These may include, but may not be limited to:

1. Limited time - free download offers for Keith's future books
2. Limited time - free download offers for other publications that we have negotiated.
3. First look previews and sample chapters of Keith's upcoming books
4. First look at articles and blog posts that Keith publishes.

Other Books By Keith Maderer:

Please check out my other print and ebooks on **Amazon.com**, my Audiobooks on **Audible.com** and online courses on **Udemy.com**. (coming soon)

Life Insurance... Who Needs It?
What Life Insurance Agents may not tell you... but YOU need to know... Before you buy
http://amazon.com/author/keithmaderer

Simplify Your Estate – The Simple Problem Solvers
Common Sense Problem Solving Strategies for Baby Boomers... and their parents
https://www.amazon.com/dp/B01LXKLOM2

How Much House... Can I Really Afford?
Practical Tips to Avoid becoming "House Poor"
https://www.amazon.com/dp/B01FQ8RL0W

Simplify Your Estate – Basic Documents
Common Sense Estate Planning Solutions
http://www.amazon.com/dp/B009F4LXE4

How To Get Your College Education... For Less
Help Design Your Own Financial Aid Package
http://www.amazon.com/dp/1453820531

Your Opinion Matters:

You are the only one that can let me know if this book is helping you with your decisions and search for the best life insurance. I truly appreciate that you decided to purchase, read and act upon this information.

I have one small request. If you would kindly write a short positive review for this book on Amazon.com, it will help me to make changes, answer additional questions and offer further valuable solutions on this an other topics.

Please let me know specifically about the selection process, common pitfalls, online resources as well as any other items you found useful.

If you click the link below it will take you to Amazon where you can sign in and share your thoughts about this book. Thank you for your effort on my behalf. I truly appreciate your time and effort.

Please Click Here to Review:

Life insurance ... Who Needs It - http://amazon.com/author/keithmaderer

Then sign in to your Amazon account, select the book to review, write and post your review.

Your Review could be the deciding factor to help someone decide to purchase this book and avoid some costly mistakes. Please share your thoughts.

Thank You.

Please Share on Social Media

Please feel free to share this book with friends, family and coworkers on Facebook, Twitter, Pinterest, Google+ or LinkedIn. Only by your word of mouth can indie authors like myself build a following that can help shape future projects and help others succeed and avoid these mistakes.

Just Copy and Paste this Text and Link below – **Thank you**

I just read this book – Great information for anyone considering life insurance - http://amazon.com/author/keithmaderer

Facebook Share - Click Here

Twitter Share – Click Here

Pinterest Share – Click Here

Google+ Share – Click Here

LinkedIn Share – Click Here

www.ingramcontent.com/pod-product-compliance
Lightning Source LLC
Chambersburg PA
CBHW070359190526
45169CB00003B/1049